FOR ANNE FRANK

FOR ANNE FRANK

Paintings by Greg Tricker
&
Poems by Nick Naydler

LOXWOOD STONELEIGH
Bristol

First published by Loxwood Stoneleigh in 1991

Printed in Great Britain by Doveton Press Ltd, Bristol
Bound by Paperback Binders, Abingdon
Cover designed by Greg Tricker
Photograph of Greg Tricker by Keith Tricker
Photograph of Nick Naydler by George Platts

An original limited edition etching complementary to each painting is available from the artist (tel: 0272 - 332910).

British Library Cataloguing in Publication Data
Tricker, Greg
For Anne Frank.
I. Title II. Naydler, Nick
821.914

ISBN 1-85125-015-2

All the titles in inverted commas are taken from *The Diary of Anne Frank*, and are used with the permission of Vallentine, Mitchell & Co. Ltd.

Loxwood Stoneleigh
11 Colston Yard, Colston Street, Bristol BS1 5BD, England

To the innocent children who died

G.T.

'A little piece of blue heaven surrounded by clouds'

In this squall of hiding,
in these abandoned rooms,
amidst this airy catacomb
do I mark the chrysalis dissolve
of childhood; writing to blue heaven
my song-chattering heart of joys
do I sing labyrinth of my heart,
do I drink through dusty windows
the world beloved, longed for;
hunted, I yet unfold.

'I hope I shall be able to confide in you'

Into you shall I plunge,
I the menagerie of girlhood;
unfurl the chorus of my life –
these secrets let me hurl
upon your white hearing;
I who am schoolgirl and quarry
clown and child, mirror and need.

'I am young and I possess many buried qualities'

Young still I yet possess
these songbirds;
I call, I name and touch,
my words fly,
my worlds shift
cleave and reveal
these landscapes, starry skies
of light and growing disclose;
in this my unbounded I am,
from this small cage, in this myself
loved creatures are always born –
this – oh beauty – I, thirteen possess.

'I am longing so longing for everything'

Everything I long for
longs for me to live; I feel
and life feels my heart
of longing and joy
forms who I am;
my laughter makes birdsong,
my wide eyes make light,
my arms are for friendship;
so I long for this everything
I am beginning.

'Spring is awakening'

I burgeoning am of mind,
my body moves and feels
to leave these child years;
I dance the spring,
light plays an ocean still unsailed;
I breathe hope, I dream life,
I run beyond my past,
my colours are a prism
in white wings and air.

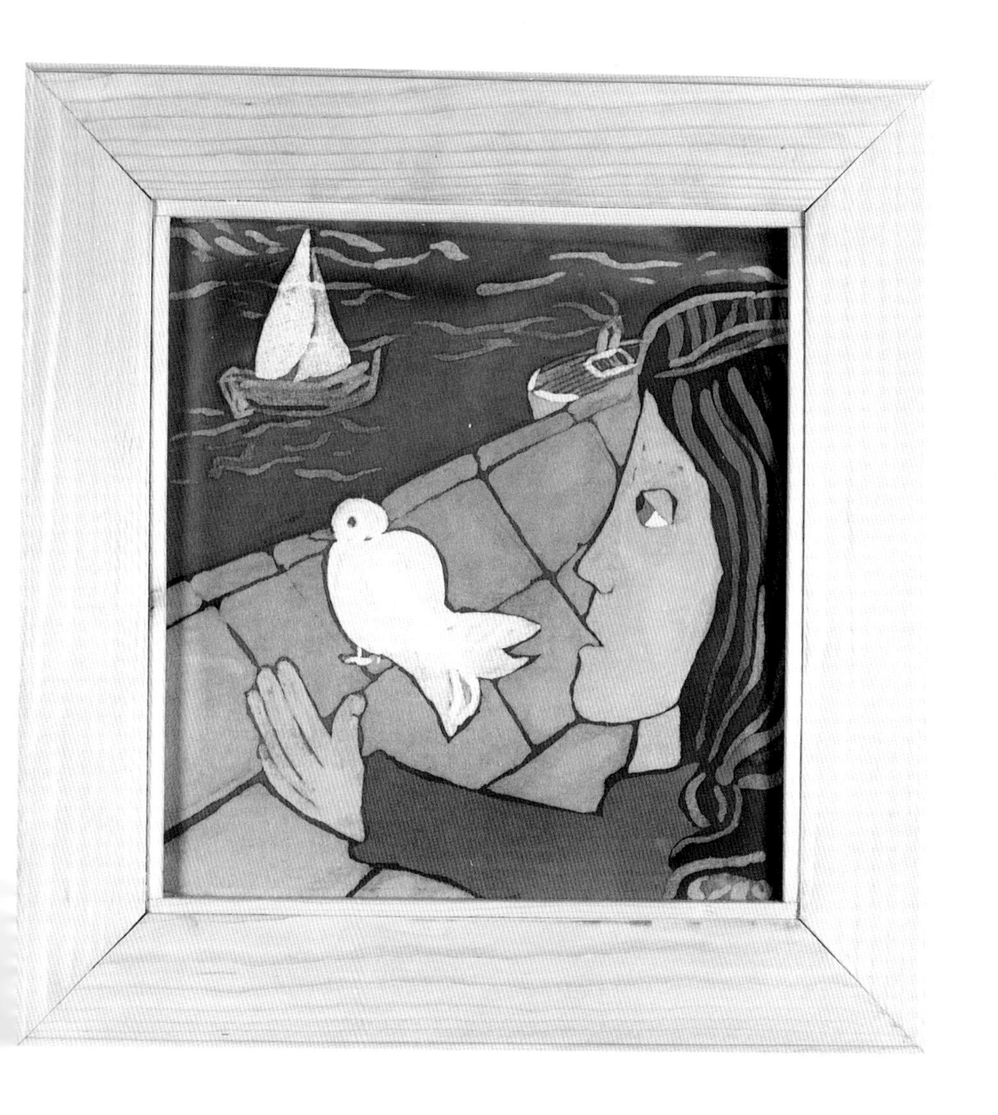

'Spring within me'

Here I run always
of legs and thoughts a whir,
of waters, fountain,
and quayside of becoming;
here do I blossom
do I promise fruits yield;
my sap astir, marked by the moon
all of fourteen I become.

'Like a songbird in its cage'

Here do I take pen
in this my cave of light,
this cage of heaven and hell,
in here unreel my life. I know
what is inside this jail;
this chapel my song is dawnlight;
I must sing.

'The lovely vase'

This lovely vase of flowers
is autumn, touches me
places I don't know where;
I dance and the music
draws a curtain from these yellow flowers falling;
world beautiful of gods I see through windows
reaches me inside.

'It is so peaceful at the moment'

Up here even
and we are, and here
alone a moment,
and all is still;
this I commit
at the altar of my diary,
these words commune –
all that in this dusk I thank,
in this confinement pray
these my wishes be ordained;
my father good, I am at peace in this moment –
be always, ever of this born.

‘We sat around the table and waited’

We are prey
and hide against the wall our lives;
candle quiet we wait,
we flee in here, eke hope
from hearts compact;
from this shared fire
we turn to this holy.

'I believe in you Peter'

I believe in you Peter –
first it seemed you were nothing –
I could feel you inward,
but silently you grew
into my growing outward; you
I daily knew through the passages of sharing
secretfuls, and by day and day
you seemed less, and were more you.
I turned and found
and there you are;
I long for the passages we reach
into one another friend,
I trust and we are us.

'Taken away by the Gestapo'

It came, the months of fear jumped
into the moment; the axe
bit deeply to the unbearable,
all dust screamed to the windows;
we turned and came unborn into the cold;
the things of our life cried out;
all torn, the night fell into my throat;
the sun fell out of my bowels.

'Loaded into cattle trucks'

All gone, the veils of my life
all pierced, the snow driven
by this undying need of a god
to take out of my nightmare this truth
and bring it through and through and through.
It leaves no air to breathe in,
no hope to crawl beside;
and snow falls on my heart.

'Let the end come'

From this violet night
a rat crawls
in the chambers of my heart;
to gnaw there
where eyes were blossom
where ears were songbird
where love was meadow;
so grows the night,
so does the end come.

'Now we are lost'

Now, in this shame we are lost;
and are all fragments
of what I can perceive
stolen into this aberration
of what childhood longed for;
what children have become
I fathom not, not see;
this pit of bestiality
has grown from what paradise
once claimed to be.

'We still hope – hope about everything'

Because this is,
with no hope allowed,
no light to dart across this sorrow –
we hope;
do we who have left no chance breach of fate
look into the eye of rodents –
to catch reflections of a light
still arbitrary in homage;
do we glimpse about everything,
against all deluge of a starless world,
this glistening of the unfathomed.

'So far away'

So far away has broken so;
from these memories
what flowered is killed;
do I stand despite this abbatoir
of what need and love sought;
do I touch what fragment,
do I see across so stormed a world,
I catch no word of what, once was;
I can but reach of selfhood
what is left in stony paths.

'The whole globe is waging war'

Such men must cry
and children die in darkest grief;
will all through fear and battle
come to this moment
beyond where beauty dwells,
deep within eyes which see such love,
through such a pit,
will all in the moment of forgiveness
be released?

Anne Frank died March 1945

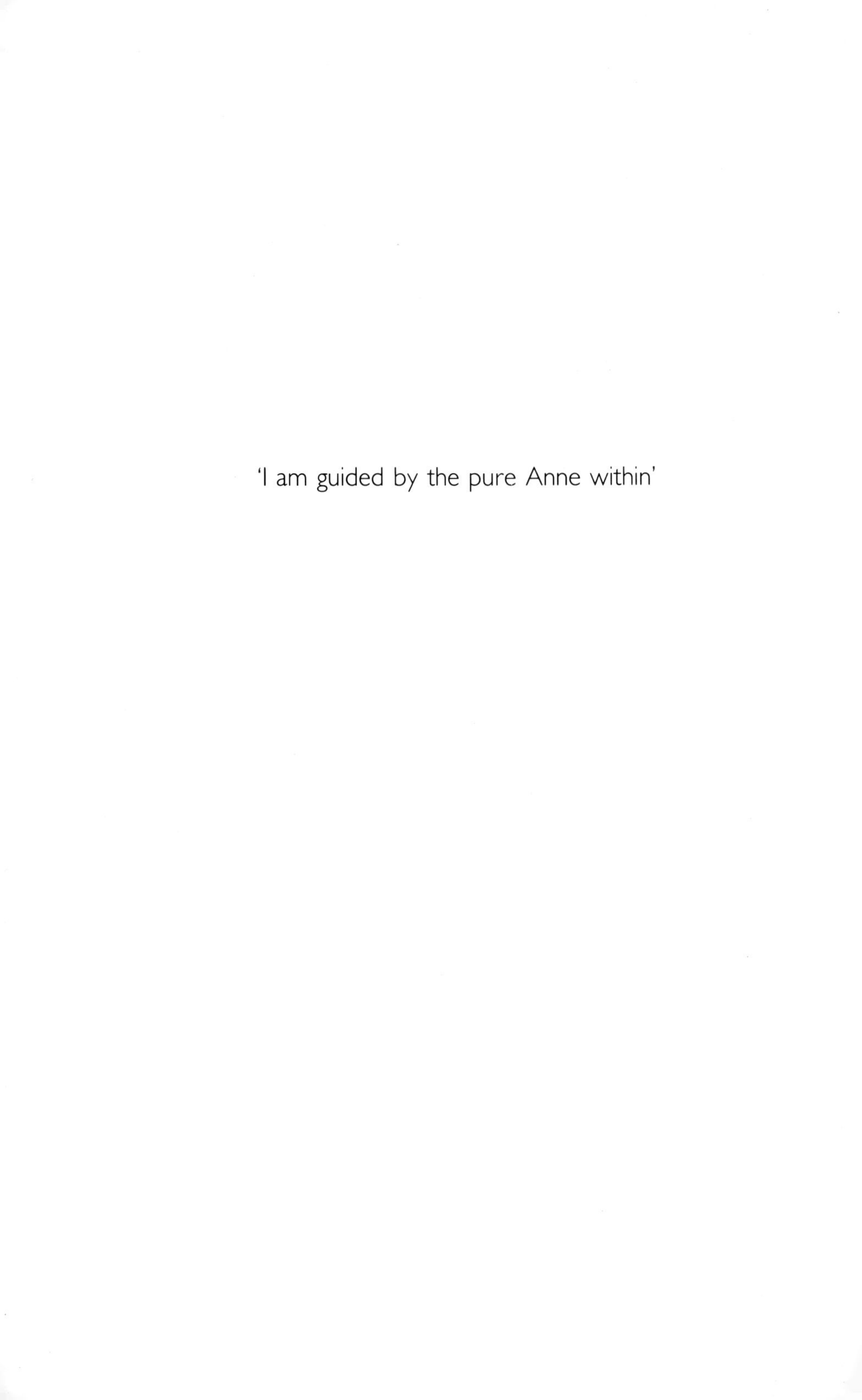

'I am guided by the pure Anne within'

'I want to go on living even after my death'

Such song I feel in these cathedrals of my heart,
such dance this chorus growing of love,
and the world so much to sing.
No death can stop such praise I feel;
not time wear thin this
radiance of breath and blood.

ARTIST'S NOTE

Like being discovered in an old dusty attic, the collection of paintings came to light one by one. Thanks to Keith, my devoted brother who exhibited them nationally, and to Rory Valentine who uniquely framed them.

G.T.